ANCIENT BRITAIN

BRENDA WILLIAMS

Publication in this form copyright © Jarrold
Publishing 2006.
Text copyright © Jarrold Publishing.
The moral right of the author has been asserted.
Series editor Angela Royston.
Edited by Clare Collinson.
Designed by Nick Avery.
Cover designed by Simon Borrough.
Picture research by Felicity Harvey.

The publishers would like to thank Dr Caroline
Malone, University of Cambridge, for reading
the text.

A CIP catalogue for this book is available from
the British Library.

Published by:
Jarrold Publishing
Healey House, Dene Road, Andover, Hampshire,
SP10 2AA
www.britguides.com

Set in Minion.
Printed in Singapore.

ISBN-10: 1 84165 165 6
ISBN-13: 978 1 84165 165 1   1/06

 Pitkin is an imprint of Jarrold
Publishing, Norwich.

CONTENTS

THE TEXTURE OF TIME

'The night of time far surpasses the day …'

Sir Thomas Browne (1605–82), Urn Burial

TOOLS FOR ALL SEASONS
Flint axes were multi-purpose tools; these are from the late Palaeolithic period (Old Stone Age). The flint was hand-held when being shaped and when used for chopping or cutting. Flint tools occur at many sites, especially those occupied by the hunters who spread through Britain after the last Ice Age.

BRONZE-AGE RELIC
New technology in the form of improved 'Beaker-style' pottery and metal weapons signifies the Bronze Age. Shown here is a typical beaker from a burial at Winterslow in Wiltshire.

DAWN OF HISTORY
Here (left), 6,000 years ago, farmers in Britain lived at the place now known as Avebury. The stone circles and earth mounds they built to link their lives to the cycles of the universe remain their memorial.

MODERN BRITAIN FORMS a short episode in the tale of the British Isles, for most of the story took place in the ancient past. Go back 9,000 years or so, and 'Britain' is not yet an island at all, but an offshoot of Europe's thinly inhabited virgin land-mass. Today's North Sea had long been a marshy plain trekked by bands of wandering hunters. Even when, around 6500 BC, rising oceans turned Britain into a 'sea-girt isle', the land would have looked unfamiliar to us. Humans were few and far between: only scattered clearings and drifting fire smoke marked their presence.

Yet people had lived in this land for thousands of years, and traces of them remain – bones and stone tools, scattered remnants of settlements, unique art. Ancient Britain has more visible monuments too: mounds, standing stones, burial barrows and hill forts. But such relics often conceal more than they reveal. We know very little about the people who built them. Their technologies were different, though they were highly skilled, and their social structures were more closely harmonized with the natural world.

With no written record to tell its story, the prehistoric past remained a mystery to the modern mind until 'antiquarians' began taking an interest in the 1500s. King Henry VIII appointed John Leland to 'search after England's antiquities' – which meant burrowing in libraries for old manuscripts, rather than in the ground for old bones. 'It would be a great profit to students and an honour to this realm,' Leland wrote of his task. Sir Thomas Browne and John Aubrey in the 17th century found the distant past equally fascinating. In Norfolk, Browne excavated 'sepulchrall urnes' which he thought were Roman but were actually Anglo-Saxon. Even so, for most God-fearing people, 'prehistory' did not exist. Archbishop Ussher (1581–1656) had decided on Biblical evidence that God created the world in 4004 BC. And that was that.

Undeterred, enthusiastic amateurs of early archaeology did fieldwork for fun;

> *'How these curiosities would be quite forgot, did not such idle fellows as I am put them down …'*
>
> John Aubrey (1625–97), historian, biographer and antiquarian

A RARE TREASURE

The Rillaton gold cup, dating from 1700–1500 BC, is one of Ancient Britain's most glittering treasures. Now in the British Museum, it came from a grave discovered in Cornwall in 1837. Other finds reported from the same grave disappeared – an all too frequent occurrence.

they dug up bones and flint tools, displaying them in the collections they created, sketched barrows and standing stones, and dug (usually in vain) for buried treasure left by the 'ancients'. While debating the origins of Stonehenge or Avebury, scholars imagined the cultures that had created such unfathomable mysteries, filling in the blanks with colourful speculation.

The term prehistory (for periods before written records began) first circulated in the 19th century, as archaeology became a serious science. New methods for dating long-buried objects, and for uncovering the texture of time, layer by layer, help us appreciate the achievement of our ancestors and the need to conserve the often fragile legacy they left. Britain possesses some of Europe's most remarkable prehistoric sites. These are the signposts that direct us into the past. An intriguing detective story puts flesh on bare bones as archaeologists interpret clues ranging from flakes of flint, deer antlers, broken pottery and rusted iron swords to

THREE AGES OF MAN

The division of prehistory into Stone, Bronze and Iron Ages was suggested in 1836 by Christian Thomsen of Denmark, but modern scholars are less happy with such rigid partitions of human development. For example, Stone-Age people used bone and antler tools too; metal-using peoples did not at once abandon older technologies; and the rate of 'progress' varied from place to place. Bronze (an alloy of copper and tin first made in the Middle East) had reached Britain by around 2300 BC. Iron, first used in Asia Minor and China, reached north-west Europe, including Britain, by around 700 BC.

brooding, moss-covered stones and windswept, grassy mounds.

This story of Ancient Britain begins millions of years ago in the dinosaur age. It continues through thousands of years of human activity, from woolly mammoth-hunting through farming, megalith-building and metal-using, until Britain emerges as part of political Europe, a province of the Roman Empire.

NEOLITHIC MARKET?

The Trundle in West Sussex is one of a number of ringed enclosures, possibly meeting places, made by farming people in the late Stone Age around 3300 BC. There were flint mines not far away, so people may have come here to trade tools and ideas.

BURIED BUCKET

An Iron-Age wooden bucket with bronze decoration and handles, found in a British grave from the period of the Roman landing led by Julius Caesar in 55 BC.

BRITAIN BEGINS

'Hands, tooth and nail, and stones were the ancient weapons; branches ripped from forests, flame and fire, once they were known …'

The Roman writer Lucretius, 1st century BC

ROMANS SUCH AS LUCRETIUS had to rely mainly on folk-memory and oral tales to guide them about 'ancient times'. Literature preserved some of the world's past history, but the rest was locked in legend, myth and baffling monuments like the pyramids of Egypt.

Antiquarians in Britain had from the 1500s begun to research studiously into the past, and by the 19th century, evolutionary theory and fossil discoveries were suggesting that the Earth had a much older history. Historians began to think in terms of 'ages', lasting many thousands of years. As scientists delved into the earth, a new picture emerged of a past before humankind, presenting scenes of climate change – including, most dramatically, the ice ages – and strange extinct creatures. Evidence for prehistoric humans later prompted widespread speculation about the life led by these early cave dwellers and hunters of giant mammoths.

Later archaeologists pinpointed developments more clearly, declaring that simple pebble tools had been made in Africa over two million years ago, beginning in the Palaeolithic period. Britain, not then an island, had its landscape and vegetation shaped by successive ice ages and warmer spells before being settled by people over 500,000 years ago. They were hunters, making flint cutters and scrapers, and other tools from antler, bone and ivory. They used

campsites, and caves in which they drew on the walls.

To explore Ancient Britain we rely on archaeologists, botanists, geographers and geneticists. To their data we can add imagination, to conjecture from fragmentary clues a picture of prehistoric life. Science has shown how closely related are many modern Britons to their distant ancestors. And we understand more clearly their relationship with the environment, as they shaped and reshaped the land, creating landmarks that still survive and patterns of settlement that we still follow.

Britain's earliest history is traced through fossils. Such remains show it was inhabited by the most exotic beasts in the Earth's menagerie, creatures that retain a unique power to fascinate, many millions of years after their extinction: the dinosaurs.

A VERY DIFFERENT KENT
A waterhole at Swanscombe in Kent, before the chill of the last Ice Age.

A GORGE FULL OF BONES
Cox's Cave, at Cheddar in Somerset, is named after George Cox, a watermill owner who ran a tea garden for tourists and whose workmen discovered the cave in 1837. In 1890 Cox's nephew Richard Gough found Gough's Cave, which in 1903 revealed 9,000-year-old 'Cheddar Man', the oldest complete skeleton found from prehistoric Britain.

A LAND OF DINOSAURS

A FIRST IN BRITAIN
Megalosaurus was the first dinosaur to be named, by William Buckland, who examined bones found at the quarry village of Stonesfield near Oxford. The Jurassic beast was a fearsome predator, 9 metres (29 feet) long from nose to tail.

THE EARTH IS 4,600 MILLION years old, but animal life has wriggled and crawled on the planet for less than 600 million years. Scientists split this vast expanse of time into three periods: the Palaeozoic ('ancient life'), the Mesozoic ('middle life') – the time of the dinosaurs – and the Cenozoic ('modern life'), from around 66 million years ago, when flowering plants, mammals, birds and humans appeared.

Mesozoic Britain, 130 million years ago, lay partly beneath the sea. Warm waters covered the ground where London now rises, and the ocean teemed with fish, molluscs and crustaceans. On shore lived dinosaurs such as *Iguanodon*, *Diplodocus* and *Megalosaurus*, roaming over land that was mostly low-lying and marshy, with lagoons around which crocodiles basked.

When prehistoric animals died, their bones were occasionally preserved as fossils, encased in rock for millions of years until exposed by erosion or dug up accidentally. Fossils were a puzzle to scientists from the time of the ancient Greek Aristotle, who studied them. When fossil hunters or farmers dug up such remains, they usually ascribed them to 'dragons' or to animals drowned in the Biblical Flood. In 1677, Dr Robert Plot, compiling a book on the natural history of Oxfordshire, decided that a reptilian thigh bone before him must have come from a human giant! In 1824, the geologist William Buckland described some similar bones, also from Oxfordshire. He declared them to be *Megalosaurus*, an extinct 'giant reptile' – and thereby caused a scientific sensation.

Further proof that giant reptiles had once roamed prehistoric Britain came from the fossil hunter Mary Anning, who found *Ichthyosaurus* in Dorset, and from Gideon and Mary Mantell, who discovered *Iguanodon* in Sussex. By 1841, fossils of at least five other species had been discovered, and the geologist Sir Richard Owen

PREHISTORIC PRINTS
*Fossilized footprints are some-
times preserved in the mud or
sand across which dinosaurs
plodded. This print, about 135
million years old, comes from
a Purbeck Stone quarry near
Swanage, Dorset.*

coined the name 'dinosaur' ('terrible reptile') for them. He was soon helping to design life-size models based, somewhat fancifully, on the scanty fossil evidence. Dinosaur fever was sparked off, and before long every local museum in Britain was striving to exhibit a bone or tooth from a long-dead local resident!

And so it has continued. In 1983, amateur fossil hunter William Walker unearthed a claw over 30 centimetres (1 foot) long, from a Surrey clay-pit. Named 'Superclaw' by newspapers, but *Baryonyx* ('heavy claw') by scientists, this animal, over 3 metres (10 feet) high and about 2 tonnes in weight, probably used its hook-like claw to scoop fish from pools and rivers.

Notable examples of prehistoric wildlife have appeared in Scotland and been eagerly greeted by the media: fossilized footprints plus the bones of 'Dougie the Dinosaur' from the Isle of Skye, and 'Lizzie the Lizard' from East Kirkton. Sadly, repeated investigations of Loch Ness have so far failed to provide proof that its legendary monster is, as some supporters have claimed, a survivor from prehistoric times.

FOSSILIZED FISH HOOK
*Some dinosaurs were special-
ized hunters. It is suggested
that* Baryonyx *used this huge
claw to catch fish, hooking
them from the water.*

SOUTH DOWNS FOSSIL HUNTER

Gideon Mantell (1790–1852) of Lewes, Sussex, was a doctor by profession and a keen fossil hunter. He announced the discovery of a dinosaur he named *Iguanodon* ('iguana tooth') in 1825, three years after publishing his first book, *Fossils of the South Downs or Illustrations of the Geology of Sussex*, which included drawings of rocks and fossils by his wife Mary.

THE FIRST BRITONS

'I can trace my ancestry back to a proto-plasmal primordial atomic globule ...'

W.S. Gilbert (1836–1911), The Mikado

HUNTERS ON FOOT
Palaeolithic hunters pursue a deer, in this painting by Maurice Wilson. These were people of the same type (Homo heidelbergensis) as those living at Boxgrove and Swanscombe.

DINOSAURS DISAPPEARED from the Earth 65 million years ago. Our human ancestors first wandered the plains of Africa over two million years ago. The process by which *Homo habilis* ('handy man') evolved into *Homo erectus* ('upright man') and later to *Homo sapiens* ('thinking man'), spreading worldwide, is still not clear, but most experts agree that human beings were living in southern Europe by 800,000 years ago.

Flint tools found near Lowestoft in Suffolk are evidence of humans in Britain 700,000 years ago – the earliest in northern Europe. Around 500,000 years ago, Palaeolithic hunters were camping around Boxgrove in West Sussex. Small groups wandered across Britain, and over what is now the North Sea, following migrating herds of deer and horses, and returning every season to favourite campsites.

Another 250,000 years later, and 'Swanscombe man' was hunting his way along the Thames and the nearby river valleys. Skull remains of a female, from the same human sub-species as the

ESSEX MAN'S TOOLKIT
Flint tools, of the style known as Clactonian (from Clacton in Essex), found at Swanscombe in Kent. Tools evolved in the Palaeolithic from simple pebbles to pear-shaped hand-axes, choppers and scrapers with carefully flaked edges.

Boxgrove people, were discovered in Swanscombe, Kent, in 1935–36. Amazingly, a matching fragment from the same skull appeared 20 years later, in 1955.

Prehistoric hunters had to be hardy to survive the perils of a nomadic hunting life. The glacial cold of the Ice Age that began to grip Europe around 150,000 years ago made survival even tougher for people with only rough shelters and caves to protect them from arctic winters.

Around 40,000 years ago, at least two species of humans were living in Europe: one was *Homo sapiens* (more or less modern people); the others were Neanderthals (named after a valley in Germany, where their remains were found in 1856). Neanderthal remains have been found in Wales, and in Norfolk where woolly mammoth and rhino bones, hand-axes and worked flints from around 50,000 years ago unearthed at Thetford in 2002 are believed to be Neanderthal-linked. Contrary to earlier theories, Neanderthals are now thought to have been at least as intelligent as *Homo sapiens.* They used flint tools, knew fire and buried their dead. Although hardy enough to survive the Ice Age, they did not live throughout it, for by 30,000 years ago they had died out, leaving the way clear for modern humans.

THE PILTDOWN HOAX
'... men quarrying in a deep gravel pit turned up a human skull ... by far the earliest trace of mankind that has yet been found in England.'
The Manchester Guardian, 21 November 1912

In 1912, a skull allegedly found at Piltdown in Sussex caused a sensation. 'Piltdown Man' was hailed as the 'missing link' between apes and humans. But in 1953 the skull was revealed as a fake, a composite of orang-utan and medieval human bones. Suspicion for the hoax has been directed at several people, including Martin Hinton, a junior scientist at the Natural History Museum in London, and local solicitor Charles Dawson (1864–1916), after whom *Eoanthropus dawsoni* ('Dawson's dawn man') was at first named.

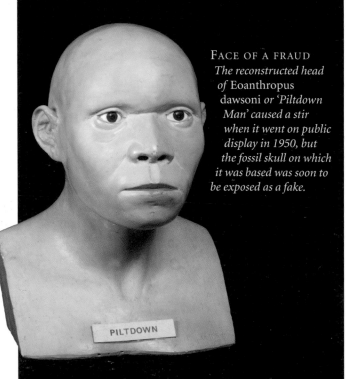

FACE OF A FRAUD
The reconstructed head of Eoanthropus dawsoni *or 'Piltdown Man' caused a stir when it went on public display in 1950, but the fossil skull on which it was based was soon to be exposed as a fake.*

PILTDOWN

STONE-AGE SUSSEX

'We get snapshots of events preserved in time …'

Dr Matt Pope, archaeologist at University College London, on the Boxgrove site

THE EARLIEST BRITONS
The Boxgrove campsite, as it probably looked 500,000 years ago. Hunters camped beside the waterhole close to the sea, yet fish is absent from their food remains. These people were ancestors of modern humans, but an earlier species, Homo heidelbergensis.

AROUND 500,000 YEARS AGO, on a beach beside chalk cliffs in Sussex, people gathered every year by a spring-fed waterhole. Rhinoceros, horse, red deer and bison came to the pool to drink. And following these browsers loped the carnivores: lion, lynx, leopard, hyena, wolf. The humans, too, were hunters, tracking the animals that were their prey.

That ancient waterhole, rediscovered thousands of years later in a gravel quarry at Boxgrove, not far from

Chichester, provided an amazing record of early human activity in Britain. Here Palaeolithic hunters camped, building shelters of branches and animal skins, and busily made tools, scattering debris around them. This prehistoric debris is treasure trove for archaeologists. Preserved by a covering of windblown sand and silt were 450 flint hand-axes as well as antler tools, thousands of animal bones, and a fragmentary trace of humanity: part of a shinbone from a left leg and two front teeth.

The animal bones show clear marks of butchery with sharp tools. Boxgrove people made tools on site, by 'knapping' – striking off flakes from a chunk of flint with a flint hammer or an antler pick. Toolmakers squatted at their work, scattering flint fragments around their feet; eight separate 'scatters' of flint were found around the carcass of a butchered horse. Hand-axes, choppers and scrapers – the basic do-it-all tools of prehistoric times – required a lot of skill to shape. Prehistoric toolmakers knew their craft and few clumsily made tools turn up.

And what were these hunters like? The leg bone found at Boxgrove came from a strongly built man around 1.8 metres (6 feet) tall. He had to be fit to hunt his prey. How he hunted is not known, although marks on a horse bone suggest a spear wound, and wooden spears have been found at other sites. Hunters almost certainly worked in small groups, stalking an old or sick animal or driving frightened deer or wild horses into an ambush. Scavenging from a lion's kill was a risky, though useful, option.

Having dragged a carcass back to camp, the butchers worked fast. Nothing was wasted. They stripped off skin, antlers and sinews, smashed bones to extract the marrow, and stored leftover meat out of reach of foxes and hyenas.

BOXGROVE TODAY
The Boxgrove site in West Sussex has excited the interest of archaeologists since its discovery in the 1980s. The detailed insights it gives into the hunting lives of early Britons have been reinforced by finds from other rare sites of similar age, such as the wooden spears – 350,000 to 400,000 years old – found at Schöningen in Germany.

THE MAN FROM BOXGROVE
Reconstruction of Boxgrove man based on the leg bone, teeth and other evidence discovered at the quarry in 1993. This Ancient Briton was a hunter, a meat-eater and a toolmaker.

HUNTER'S AXE
A flint hand-axe, one of 450 such tools found at Boxgrove. This all-purpose hunter's tool, shaped to fit the hand, was used to cut skin, flesh and bone, rather than fell trees.

CAVE PEOPLE

IN 1823, WILLIAM BUCKLAND, who later discovered *Megalosaurus*, found human bones in Goat's Hole Cave at Paviland on the Gower Peninsula in South Wales. He thought the bones were Roman and female. Animal bones in the same cave, he decided, dated from the time of Noah's Flood. Flint tools, and layers of charcoal and ash, suggested many years of human occupation.

The 'Red Lady' of Paviland became one of the stars of British prehistory. But 'she' was in fact a man, aged 25 to 30, and around 1.7 metres (just under 6 feet) tall. Radiocarbon dating showed that he was no Roman, but a Stone-Age Briton who had died about 26,000 years ago.

Buried with him were a bracelet of mammoth tusk ivory, a pendant made from a periwinkle shell, other shells, ivory rods and three spatulas made of bone. He had worn a two-piece garment and his skin had been stained with red ochre. Intriguingly, his head had been removed: either before he was buried or possibly later by scavengers or by the sea washing into the cave.

The Red Lady was an almost modern man – a human of the type known to science as Cro-Magnon after a site in southern France where specimen bones were found. Cro-Magnon people were perhaps slightly bigger than us, with bigger brains. The Goat's Hole Cave

BURIED WITH CEREMONY
The Paviland Cave burial, with the objects placed beside the dead man, suggests a ceremonial devised by people with a belief system. This reconstruction shows the funeral scene some 26,000 years ago.

CHEDDAR CAVES
Cheddar Gorge caves in Somerset have provided some of the most intriguing evidence of our links with the prehistoric past.

seems, if radiocarbon dating is accurate, to have been occupied for some 3,000 years, and was possibly a sacred burial site, commanding a majestic view when the sea was further away and at a lower level than today. But what was the significance or use of the ivory rods and bone spatulas left beside the corpse? In the 21st century we no longer have the 'keys' to understanding such details: we can only speculate.

It was not long after the Paviland burial that the final stage of Britain's last Ice Age began, around 18,000 years ago. Milder and colder spells succeeded one another, until the final warming that set in around 13,000 years ago. Intense cold made life much more difficult for humans. Those who did not migrate south sought shelter in caves, using them as ceremonial sites and burial places. Caves therefore provide valuable 'snapshots' into prehistory. The Cheddar caves of Somerset show evidence of 40,000 years of human occupation, and Britain's oldest complete skeleton (9,000 years old) was found in one of them, Gough's Cave, in 1903.

Gough's Cave produced fresh surprises in 1986, when new bones came to light: the remains of at least three adults and two children, jumbled among flints, antlers, bits of ivory and animal bones. Cut marks on the human bones show that the corpses had been dismembered after death. Stone-Age Britons may have exposed their dead in the air for scavengers (as Indian Parsees and some Native Americans did) before the bones were dealt with. Or they may have disjointed the corpses as part of the funeral practice, before laying the bones carefully to rest in sacred spots. Cannibalism for ritual purposes is another possibility.

BRITAIN'S OLDEST BURIAL
A thigh bone from the headless man buried at Paviland. His is the oldest known burial of a 'modern human' in Britain.

CRESWELL CAVE ART

ARTIST AT WORK
Church Hole in Derbyshire, as it might have appeared 12,000 years ago. An artist engraves the rock wall using a sharpened flint point tool called a burin.

CAVES OFFERED STONE-AGE PEOPLE refuge from bad weather in winter, but were also places to commune with the personal and spirit world through art. By the light of lamps burning animal fat, or faint sunshine from the cave mouth, artists painted or scratched images of the animals that shared their world. In 2003, Britain's oldest prehistoric rock-art was discovered on the walls of a cave at Creswell Crags, Derbyshire.

Creswell Crags, a limestone gorge not far from Sheffield, harbours a number of deceptively named caves: among them Mother Grundy's Parlour, Robin Hood's Cave, The Pin Hole and Church Hole.

When revealed, the newly identified rock engravings from Creswell were hailed by the news media as 'Britain's oldest cave art' and comparable to the famous cave paintings at Lascaux in France or Altamira in Spain. The Creswell engravings were rather faint, which is perhaps unsurprising after so long a time. Dated by measuring traces of uranium in the limestone crust that had formed over them, the pictures proved to have been created 12,800 years ago. This made the Creswell drawings at least 6,000 years older than any other known British rock art, if a little younger than the 14,000-year-old works at Lascaux.

Creswell Crags is 'the most northerly place on the planet where cave art from this period has been found', according

'… like waking up one morning and finding the Mona Lisa on your garage door …'

Dr Nigel Mills, Creswell Heritage Trust, on the rock engravings

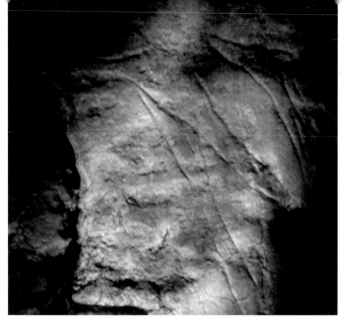

BIRDS OR WOMEN?
Seen by some as birds, and by others as emblematic women, these engravings may alternatively be geometric shapes.

to Jon Humble, English Heritage's inspector of ancient monuments for the area. At Creswell Crags, cave artists made skilful use of uneven rock surfaces, creating superbly realistic outlines of ibex, bison, goat, part of a horse, and birds (though some critics interpret the 'birds' as 'dancing women'). Earlier visitors had considered the faint lines on the cave walls as graffiti, to which some had added their own details – a beard drawn on the ibex, and the date '1940' scratched on the goat, which also bore someone's initials on its rump.

CRAGS FROM THE AIR
With the discovery of its cave art, Creswell Crags has become one of the most significant prehistoric sites in Britain.

RIDDLES OF THE NORTH

Later in date than Creswell's cave pictures, but more numerous, are the 'cup and ring' rock engravings of Northumberland. More than 1,000 of these abstract designs were cut into rocks between 6,000 and 3,500 years ago, and new examples are still being found on farms and moorland. Why the images were made, and what lies behind them, remains a mystery.

Herds and flocks

Unique white cattle
The Chillingham Park cattle have been enclosed for many centuries in their home in Northumberland. They may be descended from the aurochs or another species of wild cattle.

Soay sheep
The first sheep herded in Britain probably resembled the Soay breed of the Western Isles. Sheep are not native to Britain, so all farmed stock has been bred from imported species.

FROM HAMBLEDON HILL in Dorset and other parts of the south-west comes evidence of cattle-rearing, for the first British farmers raised beef as well as barley. Domestic cattle were introduced to Britain from Continental Europe, along with grain and pulses (beans and peas). Cattle and horses had long been hunted for meat, and now in the third millennium BC, people began to herd them. The Exmoor pony is thought to be the native British horse; perhaps hunters brought home young animals, orphaned when their mothers were killed, and then hand-reared them to form the nucleus of a domestic herd.

The domestic cattle in Britain were long-horns, smaller and less aggressive than the native wild aurochs and almost

certainly 'imported'. It is likely that there was an autumn cull to provide winter meat (and a feast), and most cattle were slaughtered for meat when they were between two and three years old. So began a long-lasting tradition of British beef-eating, for later Bronze- and Iron-Age Britons also kept large herds of cattle. Besides meat, cattle provided hides for leather, sinews, horn and bones. Evidence of milk-fat residues on Neolithic pottery shows that people began to add dairy products to their diet, too.

Sheep and goats, also probably intro-duced to Britain, were hardy enough to be herded in most parts of the country, providing wool and milk, as well as meat. Prehistoric sheep were small, wiry animals, something like the Soays of

smaller than a modern porker, closer in looks to the wild boar. It may have been bred from the European wild pig, but could also have been an import, descended from Middle-Eastern breeds. For nomadic people, the pig had a major drawback: it was not a long-distance traveller, whereas cattle, sheep and goats all wandered naturally between summer and winter pastures. But the pig was well suited to the more settled way of life developing, especially in southern Britain.

Dogs ran alongside hunters and herdsmen. Skeletal remains of Labrador-sized dogs date from as early as 8000 BC in Britain. These animals were probably wolf-like in appearance, the wolf being ancestor to all domesticated dogs. But bones of smaller, terrier-type animals also occur. Small dogs would have been useful as watchdogs and rat-catchers, although some were no doubt family pets, too.

WILD BOAR
The European wild boar is a formidable animal, long extinct in Britain but now ranging again in southern England, where escaped stock has run wild. The first 'domestic' pigs lived a similarly free-range existence in woodland, for at least part of the year.

St Kilda in the Hebrides, long isolated and regarded as the oldest native breed. No shearing was required, as these animals shed their fleeces naturally in early summer; 'moulting' animals could be caught and their wool plucked off by the handful. Goats, even hardier than sheep, became widespread, too.

Pork was a particular favourite at late Neolithic feasts and pigs were easy to keep in forested areas, where they could root for acorns. The Neolithic pig was

MIGHTY BIG-HORN
Part of a horn from the extinct aurochs, the wild ox of ancient British woodlands. Once common in Europe, the aurochs survived in Poland until the 1620s. It was black, with forward-curving horns, and stood 1.8 metres (6 feet) high.

VILLAGES OF STONE

*'… the most exciting prehistoric site in north-western Europe.
Everything is there … superbly preserved.'*

Francis Pryor, on Skara Brae in Orkney, from his book Britain BC

THE VILLAGE WORKSHOP?
*This building, set to one side on
the west, differs in design from
the other houses at Skara Brae.
It may have been a workshop
where stone tools were made.*

MOST NEOLITHIC HOMES were made of
organic material – wood, turf and animal
hides – which is seldom preserved. Where
trees were few and timber other than
driftwood scarce, as in Orkney and other
outlying Scottish islands, Neolithic
people built in stone. They even made
furniture of stone, so providing a price-
less record for future archaeologists.

Skara Brae is a stone 'village' in Orkney,
dating from between 3200 and 2700 BC.
It was uncovered in 1850 by a storm that
laid bare the remains of a prehistoric
settlement beneath sand dunes, and was
first excavated by a local laird, William
Watt. So far, ten dwellings have been
revealed. This late Stone-Age settlement
is rather like a commune, a series of
linked rooms within thick dry-stone
walls, probably once roofed over with
driftwood and whale bones, and covered
over with turf and bracken. The
doorways were narrow and
low, like the ceilings. Inside,
the rooms had built-in
stone furnishings that
included seats, beds,

dressers with shelves and storage niches (one still had the owner's beads in it), as well as basins lined with clay for water. The whole complex was drained by a sewer carrying discharge from individual houses. These were snug homes, in which families could take refuge from the slashing rain and biting winds of a northern winter. There do seem to have been certain rules of occupation, however. It has been suggested that the arrangement of bed ledges was divided: women and children on the left of the entrance and men on the right.

❧

People lived mainly on meat and milk from their cattle and sheep, and on shellfish, especially limpets. They made simple pottery, elaborately decorated, and also decorated the walls of their houses with scratched patterns. The people themselves wore jewellery in the form of pendants and beads made from sheep bone, cow teeth and ivory tusks. They made dice for games from walrus ivory, and played at knucklebones.

❧

The villagers of Skara Brae used what they had to hand: beach stone for building,

pebbles and animal bones for tools. Little went unused – even household rubbish. Shellfish refuse and peat ash mixed with sand was banked around some of the huts, almost concealing them so that linking alleyways became stone-roofed tunnels. This would have insulated the homes from scouring winds and hidden them from view.

❧

Ten more houses have been found at Barnhouse, 8 kilometres (5 miles) to the east, not far from the burial chamber of Maes Howe and the Stones of Stenness. One is quite large (7 metres/23 feet square), possibly a ceremonial building, but the absence of communal rubbish suggests that this settlement was not in use for anything like as long as Skara Brae.

NEOLITHIC STYLE
Living room of a Skara Brae house. Well shielded from the wind and rain, people could feel warm and secure.

PERPLEXING POLYHEDRA
Carved multi-sided balls found at Skara Brae along with pots and bone pins, necklace beads and containers of red ochre, perhaps used as face paint. Similar balls are known from other northern sites but their purpose is unknown.

TOOLMAKERS

FLINT SEAM
This is a flint seam in Canon Greenwell's Pit, with antler picks, the miner's standard tools. Later people feared that the Grimes Graves flint mines were the Devil's work (hence the name: Grim was a name later used for the Devil).

TOOLS WERE THE MOST prized currency in Ancient Britain. The basic tool was the axe, made from flint or other types of stone. Britain had at least 50 varieties of stone suitable for grinding and polishing, though the best sources were the volcanic and metamorphic hard rocks of the north and west. Far more common, though less durable, was the flint axe, especially in the south and east of Britain, where flint is found in chalk and limestone.

Stone tools, once thought necessarily rough and ready, were anything but. Toolmakers spent hours of patient labour in selecting the right flints from which to prepare half-worked 'cores' that might then be taken several days' journey away to a fresh site, for finishing. Flakes were struck off a core with a 'soft' hammer such as a deer antler. Many stone axes were probably hafted – fitted into wood or antler handles. Toolmakers used birch-bark resin to 'cement' a hollowed-out antler onto a stone axe-head, forming a handle or sleeve.

HAMMERING AWAY
Stone tools could tackle heavy jobs, as well as more delicate scraping and trimming. This stone hammer head comes from Windmill Hill, Wiltshire.

32

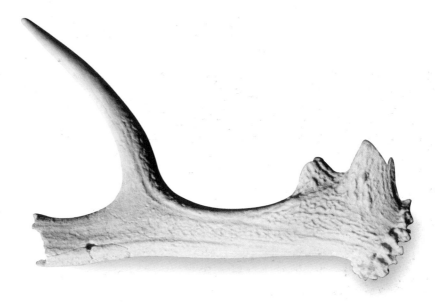

Antler and bone were almost as useful as flint. Slivers of bone were used to make pins and needles. The scapula (shoulder bone) of an ox or pig made a useful shovel or scoop. Small hollowed-out sheep bones were chopped up to make beads. Bone was also good for making barbed harpoon heads and fish hooks, while red deer antler served as a digging tool, or a hoe. The finely notched tine (tip) of an antler made a good comb.

Stone tools could kill prey, cut flesh, work leather and wood, and till the soil. Their makers skilfully created a range of shapes: axe, adze, chisel, knife, scraper, awl and bone drill, and so successful were they that everyday tools continued to be made

of stone long into the metal age. Many families preserved flint-knapping skills even after the ironsmith had begun his smoky mysteries in the forge. Less effective was the stone plough. It was not until the 1st millennium BC that iron ploughshares gave farmers extra power to tackle the heavy clay soils that had defeated their ancestors.

Wood, too, had many uses. Stone-Age hunters and farmers knew every type of tree and how to use its timber, whether for boats, ploughs, fencing, furnishings, spades, spears, harpoons, or throwing sticks for downing birds and small game. The oldest known English bows, from Somerset (*c.*3400 BC), were as tall as a man and they were made, like the medieval longbow, from yew.

BASKETS AND ROPES

Baskets were created from bendy twigs and reeds, using the same weaving technique that produced mats and sheep hurdles. Strong string or rope could be made from twisted heather, wild clematis and honeysuckle. Plaited rawhide took the strain of hauling heavy stones or logs.

TRACKS AND TRAVELLERS

STONE-AGE HUNTERS were used to walking long distances as they followed migrating animal herds, returning in season to places they knew to be rich in fish, fruit or game. The same trails were later followed by those more interested in axe production than chasing deer, as people trekked many miles to find tools and toolmaking materials. Most of the best flint came from the south (from Findon, near Worthing in Sussex, for instance), but there were Neolithic 'tool factories' in Cumbria, the Highlands and Norfolk. Late Neolithic polished axes, ground and smoothed into an elegant shape, were traded across Britain from Great Langdale, Cumbria, and the Preseli Hills of Wales. A stone's place of origin, as well as its beauty, gave special value: perhaps that is why the Stonehenge builders later brought their bluestones to Salisbury Plain from Preseli.

Wiltshire, so rich in prehistoric sites, lies at the centre of a network of ancient ridgeway tracks used by travellers and traders. Many converge on Salisbury Plain, following dry ridges bare of natural woodland from Cornwall to the south coast, East Anglia, the Midlands, the north of England and Wales. Ridgeways were the main long-distance prehistoric trade routes, one key path being the Harroway (Hoar, or Hard, Way) along the North Downs chalk ridge from Dover to Stonehenge. This was the main route from the Dover Strait, the land-bridge to mainland Europe until the waters closed above it.

Water was no barrier to travel. By 8,000 years ago, seafarers were crossing to islands in canoes or coracles, visiting the Scottish island of Rum, for instance, to collect the local 'bloodstone' (a form of silica) prized for making polished axes. Ireland and Britain were separated by rising sea levels some time after 7500 BC, so crossing the Irish Sea meant building log-craft or skin-boats.

Most routes were foot-trodden only, but Neolithic people did build some wooden 'roads'. In 1970, Raymond Sweet, working

THE SWEET TRACK
A section of the Sweet Track, now preserved. The pathway was made of oak, ash and lime, and the supporting rails and pegs mainly of hazel and alder.

LANGDALE PIKES
The bleakly beautiful fells of Cumbria attracted travellers eager for greenstone, from which some of the finest Neolithic axes were made.

for a peat-extraction company in Somerset, discovered a piece of wood interesting enough to send to an expert. 'The parcel contained a piece of ash plank, clearly split from a large tree,' commented John Cole of Cambridge University. The wood came from a prehistoric footpath, built to rest on timbers driven into the Somerset peat. Known as 'Sweet Track', the single-file path was 1,800 metres (about a mile) long, laid in 3807–3806 BC across boggy ground to a drier patch of land. The sections were prepared on firm ground, laid end to end and secured by pegs driven slant-wise into the ground on either side. Foot planks were wedged into

place between the peg-tops, parallel to the timber beneath, and held in position by more pegs. The whole track could have been laid in a day.

~

We know people used the Sweet Track because objects were dropped near it. A rare jadeite axe-head, thought to have come all the way from Switzerland, was found beside the path. Surely this was too precious an object to have been lost carelessly. Was it dropped deliberately in the bog, as an offering?

IMPORTED ICON
An axe-head of polished jadeite, a rare form of jade, manufactured by many hours of careful labour. Made from Italian stone, this axe must have had special value as a gift or ceremonial offering.

ONE-MAN BOAT
Stone-Age people paddled small boats such as coracles, wood-framed craft that were covered with hides. The coracle is probably the oldest form of boat in continuous use in Britain – and still being made in Wales today.

35

WINDMILL HILL

'... a very delicate hill ... the turf as soft as velvet ...'

William Stukeley, who explored Wiltshire in the 1700s

WINDMILL HILL
Windmill Hill was, like other enclosures, probably a meeting place. Here communities could exchange goods and news, barter animals, initiate young people into maturity, marry and perform rituals essential to the renewed fertility of their land.

POT LUCK
Pottery from Windmill Hill. Early Neolithic pottery was round-bottomed, and not always decorated. Later pots were made with flat bottoms, and decorative styles became more fancy.

A NEOLITHIC TRAVELLER crossing Wiltshire's Marlborough Downs would have been startled to see Windmill Hill's enormous ditches and banks. The biggest man-made features previously known would have been burial barrows, so this impressive structure had no equal in Britain – 350 metres (1,150 feet) in diameter at its outer ring, 85 metres (280 feet) at the inner. The outer ring, 2.4 metres (8 feet) deep, was dug, like the others, around 3550 BC.

Around 3800 BC, people in Britain had begun changing the landscape around them in a big way. They constructed large circular enclosures, ringed by ditches dug in segments with crossing places (causeways) in between, and from these 'bridges' came the name 'causewayed enclosures'. The ditches were dug so that excavated earth could be piled up into huge banks around the enclosures. Few remains of houses have been found, just possessions: pottery, flint tools, polished stone axes and bones. Two of the largest causewayed enclosures, or camps, are at Hambledon Hill in Dorset and Windmill Hill in Wiltshire, about 2.5 kilometres (1.5 miles) north-west of Avebury.

Any trees and scrub growing on Windmill Hill's low slopes had to be cleared before building could start. Considerable organization was required, as thousands of basket-loads of chalk were hacked from the ground. Each trench, or trench section, may have been assigned to one family-group, perhaps under the supervision of a project leader, or group of leaders. The diggers do not seem to have cared much about keeping their trenches neatly spaced: three rings of ditches are now barely visible, but they were probably once topped with timber fencing. The site's most obvious features today are later Bronze-Age barrows.

BRINGING IN
THE HARVEST
*Around Windmill Hill, and
wherever farmers planted
crops, harvest time was
crucial. People worked together
in the fields, cutting the grain
with flint-edged sickles.*

INQUIRING MIND
*William Stukeley (1687–1765)
pioneered the exploration of
ancient sites such as Windmill
Hill, Avebury and Stonehenge.
He was first secretary of the
Society of Antiquaries, founded
in 1707.*

Farmers around Windmill Hill raised cattle, grew wheat in plots and mined for flint to make their tools and weapons. They also traded with other groups of people, sometimes far afield, as they possessed types of pottery also found in France and Switzerland. One of the most unusual finds from Windmill Hill was a man buried in an oval grave. Single burials of this kind are rare in the early Neolithic period, when most people were buried in communal graves marked by barrows and cairns.

Knap Hill and Rybury are among smaller enclosures that lie near Windmill Hill, and others exist elsewhere in southern England. Some enclosures were sited on hilltops with commanding views, reached only by steep paths. Some had impressive wooden gateways made from oak beams.

These 'camps' do not appear to have been all-year settlements, but were perhaps used seasonally as stockyards for cattle corralled for market or slaughter, and gathering places where people met to celebrate, to perform rituals, or bury their dead.

Remains quarried from Windmill Hill include stone axes, flint scrapers and knives, arrowheads, antler combs and bits of pottery. Traces of hazelnuts and crab apples suggest autumnal feasts at cattle-slaughtering time. Chalk 'phalli' and cups may suggest fertility cults.

STONE DEAD

REPOSITORY FOR BONES
*The West Kennet long barrow,
restored to something like its
original appearance, when a
forecourt at the wide end was
perhaps used during burial ceremonies. Inside were found the
bones of 46 adults and children.*

THE LIVING SHARED their landscape with
the dead in Neolithic Britain, where the
bones of the dead were buried in their
own communities within megalithic
('great stone') tombs, often covered over
with earth to form a hummock or
barrow. Great stone slabs guarded the
dead in their silent mounds and dark,
chambered rock tombs.

On the southern chalklands, earth
mounds were heaped up over wooden
'death-houses', while further north and in
the west, rock chamber tombs were built:
the dolmens of Cornwall, for instance,
and the impressive passage graves of
Ireland, North Wales and Scotland. Many
tombs were altered by successive generations. Their main use was for burials
(an average of six people per tomb in
Wessex), but some barrows may have
been built originally as mortuary enclosures, where corpses were exposed to the
elements and scavengers before the bones
were laid to rest.

The building of communal long barrows
for burials was at its height between 3800
and 2800 BC; few were made after 2500 BC.
These tombs are found across Wessex and
as far north as Scotland, which has long
cairns too. Some barrows are very large,
like that at Maiden Castle in Dorset, and
the West Kennet barrow in Wiltshire,
which is 107 metres (350 feet) long, but
most barrows are between 20 metres and
80 metres (50–165 feet) in length. Some
have vanished under ploughed land;
others have been flattened, leaving only a
pit of bones where once the mound rose.

Stone chamber or passage graves were
equally numerous. Passage graves had a
corridor from the entrance to a round
burial chamber, while gallery graves
enclosed a long cavity, sometimes with
side-chambers. Britain has at least 600
stone-built tombs, more than half in
Scotland, though many more must have
disappeared over time, their stones carted
away by local builders and farmers. Most
were originally enclosed by earth or stone

walling, but often only bare slabs of stone still stand, exposed by wind and weather, like those at Zennor Quoit and Trethevy Quoit in Cornwall.

Maes Howe in Orkney and Bryn Celli Ddu in Wales were impressive mounds, concealing stone-lined passages and chambers for the bones (less often corpses), with grave goods such as pots. Maes Howe was built around 2850 BC. The tomb is 35 metres (115 feet) across and 8 metres (26 feet) high, built on a platform twice that width and enclosed by a circular ditch. Three stone slabs, each weighing 3 tonnes, form the exterior, from which a passage leading to the central chamber is angled to let the midwinter sun shed light within. No burial goods from this tomb are known – any 'treasures' it contained may have been removed by Vikings in the 1100s, who left behind inscriptions in Old Norse. To the west of Maes Howe were the 12 Stones of Stenness (of which four now remain), dating from 3040 BC, and aligned north-west to this circle is the Ring of Brodgar, surrounded by barrows. Orkney also has a rare rock-cut tomb, the Dwarfie Stane.

SATISFIED VISITOR

In 1669, Samuel Pepys stopped his coach on the way home from Chatham Dockyard to view Kits Coty House, a chambered barrow in Kent: '... **three stones standing upright and a great round one lying on them ...** not so big as those at Salisbury Plain, but **certainly it is a thing of great antiquity and I am mightily glad to see it.'**

DEVIL'S DEN
Near Marlborough in Wiltshire stands this 'dolmen', actually part of a long barrow from which the earth and stones of the original mound have vanished over the centuries.

THE RITUAL LANDSCAPE

By around 3000 BC, Britain's way of life –
and death – was being changed by the
new farming lifestyle. People following
settled lives were disposing of their dead
in 'settled' places, but as well as community tombs they began to build larger
structures of wood and stone. The most
celebrated of these is Stonehenge in
Wiltshire, though there are others,
equally astounding: the stone circles at
Callanish on the isle of Lewis and elsewhere and the gaunt stones at Avebury,
Wiltshire. Such monumental landmarks
indicate a 'ritual landscape' in Ancient
Britain, the meaning of which has
aroused speculation ever since people
began to study ancient stones – rather
than cart them away for use as a free
source of building material.

The more imaginative but improbable
suggestions – that some of this new
building was inspired by Mediterranean
architects, or brought to Earth by aliens
from space – add to the aura of mystery.
The achievements are evident. From the
Orkneys and Western Isles to the south-
west downlands of Wessex, impressive
remnants reveal a society in transition
between stone and metal ages.

The motivation behind the achievements
is less clear. Religion, seasonal ceremonial and more complex social structures may have been crucial. Britain was
evolving a new 'sacred geography',
ancient in its roots and reinforced
generation after generation by those
adding to or rebuilding the processional avenues and gathering places
of their ancestors. Those creating this
landscape were apparently as much
concerned with 'place' – the stone
monument's setting, its approaches,
and what could be seen from it –
as with the immense problems of
construction. They have left us some
of the most awesome and haunting
sights in Britain, ancient or modern.

THE RING-PEOPLE

IN THE LATE Neolithic–Bronze Age period, most villages lay within an easy walk of the fields, at the centre of a 'clan' territory marked by barrows and cairns. Natural features such as rivers and hills held a special spiritual significance for each clan, many of which were small extended families. Some may also have adopted a special animal 'totem' – a bull, perhaps, or red deer, dog, bird, even a seal. There is an old Orkney saying: 'I am a man on the land, and a selkie [seal] in the sea.' Animal burial cults are a possibility, too: Fussell's Lodge long barrow near Stonehenge had an ox-skin, complete with head and hoofs, draped over the gateway to the mortuary chamber. A burial mound at Irthlingborough, Northamptonshire, concealed 184 cattle skulls, perhaps relics of gifts brought by mourners.

The earthwork ring at Mount Pleasant in Dorset had a large timber stockade inside, possibly for cattle. In the south of the country, cattle had become a symbol of wealth, even though crop-growing later expanded. Did the building of grandiose structures at Durrington Walls, Avebury and Stonehenge reflect a 'top-down' social order? Not necessarily. Early Britain seems to have been fairly egalitarian, at least in the way people were buried.

DURRINGTON WALLS
Hard at work erecting the timbers of Durrington Walls, an enclosure similar to but larger than Woodhenge. At the heart of the Salisbury Plain ritual landscape, both sites held special significance for the people who built them.

BURIED BRITONS
Skeletal remains – the bones of four adults and two children, dating from around 2300 BC and found at Amesbury, Wiltshire.

By about 2000 BC, social rank is more evident in grades of burial: children, women and adolescents, men and chiefs. A chieftain, possibly elected, led the community in public works, in ritual ceremonies, and in diplomatic exchanges of gifts with neighbours. But whether he held 'kingly' rank is debatable. Rich clan-heads or chieftains showed a taste for 'gracious living' and ornament, stimulated by Wessex's trade with Ireland and Cornwall, which were key sources of tin. Trade across Europe reached as far as the Baltic, and Baltic amber worked in Wessex even found its ways into Greek graves at Mycenae.

Specialist workers such as potters and bronze-smiths did their share of communal farm work. So presumably did priests, guardians of ritual and seasonal ceremonial at the stone circles. At certain times of year, people assembled here from small self-governing communities typically numbering no more than 50 people. What they did at these gatherings remains conjecture, but the places to which they came were fundamental to their lives and beliefs. Following processional routes used for thousands of years, people were linking present and past, life and death.

Archaeologists have shown that work at Stonehenge began about 2800 BC and continued for some 1,700 years. However, the site itself was far more ancient. Three pits came to light at Stonehenge during 1966 excavations for a car park, and another pit in 1988. Each cavity, shaped to receive a thick pine-wood post, had been dug 10,000 years ago, between 8500 and 7650 BC!

ARCHER'S POINT
A stone arrowhead from Wessex. Bows and arrows were used for hunting, and other killings. In 1978 the remains of a Bronze-Age arrow victim, shot at least twice at close range, were found at Stonehenge.

'There is also in the island a precinct sacred to Apollo and suitably imposing, and a notable spherical temple decorated with many offerings …'

Greek historian Hecateus of Abdera (4th century BC), quoted by Diodorus Siculus, 8 BC

AVEBURY

'This old monument does as much exceed in greatness the so renowned Stonehenge as a cathedral does a parish church.'

John Aubrey, writing in the 17th century

OVER 4,000 YEARS AGO, people at Avebury in Wiltshire undertook an enormous project that still puzzles their descendants. The result – two large stone circles enclosed within a Great Circle of stones, 332 metres (1,089 feet) across – remained an important ceremonial centre for around 700 years.

About a hundred stones were originally in the Great Circle, the largest forming entrances to the north and south. Within stood two more stone circles (not fully uncovered and so now incomplete). One originally had 29 stones; the other was a double ring of 27 and 12 stones. Today, the biggest megalith left standing is the 65-tonne Swindon Stone in the outer circle. Its partner collapsed in the early 18th century, but not before William Stukeley had taken measurements that suggest it was probably larger, around 90 tonnes! Digging banks and ditches, then moving and erecting the stones was

a massive undertaking, with an estimated 120,000 cubic metres of chalk to be shifted. Local sarsen (sandstone) stones, like those at Stonehenge, were used in their natural state, untrimmed, and tests in the 1930s showed that it took 14 men four days to erect one small stone, guiding it into a shallow socket with ropes, wooden props and levers. Although the builders must have hit many snags, their skill and persistence ensured that some stones remained standing for 4,000 years,

COLD STONE
Avebury in winter, a scene showing surviving stones.

46

'With awe and diffidence I enter the sacred precincts of this once hallowed sanctuary, the supposed parent of Stonehenge, **the wonder of Britain and the most ancient,** as well as the most interesting relict which our island can produce.'

Sir Richard Colt Hoare, *Ancient Wiltshire* (1812)

resisting all efforts by later generations to remove or obliterate them.

Although a village had been on the spot for at least a thousand years in historic times, Avebury's stones remained unknown to outsiders until John Aubrey recognized their importance in 1648. In 1723, Stukeley measured the central obelisk of the south circle at 7 metres (21 feet), noting it was 'higher than the rest'. Already fallen, it was broken up a few years later. Other stones were toppled over at various times, and buried. A medieval barber-surgeon meddling with the monument had been crushed under a stone around 1325. Coins in his purse confirm the date of his death, and the 'Barber Stone' commemorates him.

Pillaged for building stone in the 17th and 18th centuries, prehistoric Avebury was dangerously near disappearing altogether by Victorian times. However, it was rescued, first by Sir John Lubbock (later Lord Avebury) who bought part of the village, and then by the marmalade millionaire Alexander Keiller, who bought the site in 1934 and re-erected many of the fallen stones.

Since John Aubrey recognized its importance, Avebury has been 'the wonder of Britain, Ireland and Brittany', according to prehistorian Aubrey Burl, but though its significance may have been generally agreed, its nature has not. Avebury was

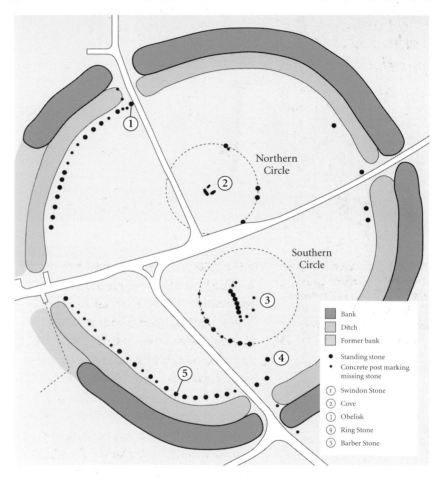

once claimed as England's first city, for example, while in 1840 the Reverend Warner suggested that it was Phoenician, as was Stonehenge. In 1883, W.S. Blacket proposed Native American origins for the stones, whereas another 19th-century writer, James Fergusson, considered that the monument marked the site of the last battle of King Arthur. In fact, this remarkable monument is many years older than any such fanciful speculations. Its date is now put at around 2600 BC.

RINGS WITHIN RINGS
Plan of Avebury showing the outer ditch and bank surrounding the two inner circles.

SILENT WITNESSES
Stonehenge today. So familiar are its fallen stones that it takes an act of imagination, or carefully simulated reconstruction, to picture the monument with its rings of stone complete.

FIRST STONES
In the long days of summer, around 5,000 years ago, people on the Wiltshire downland began to build the first Stonehenge.

AVEBURY'S ONLY RIVAL as Britain's premier ancient monument is Stonehenge. Yet today's Stonehenge is a shade of the site in its prime: the outer boundary, a ditch and low bank, once stood about 2 metres (over 6 feet) high. Cutting the boundary is the Avenue entry, plus several narrower entrances, and within the Avenue stands the Heel Stone. This 35-tonne megalith, probably hauled 36 kilometres (22 miles) from the Marlborough Downs, marks 'like a gun-sight' the alignment of the midsummer sunrise. At the entrance to the ring is the now fallen Slaughter Stone, lone survivor of three gateway stones. Discs on the ground mark 56 steep-sided round pits (the 'Aubrey Holes'), and on this circle stand two of four original Station Stones, indicating other astronomical alignments.

The outer Sarsen Circle was once a 30-stone ring, crowned by a ring of 30 lintel stones. Within is the incomplete Bluestone Circle, originally of 60 stones.

Five Sarsen Trilithons inside these circles formed a horseshoe shape, in which stood the 19 stones of the Bluestone Horseshoe. At the very heart is the Altar Stone, now buried beneath fallen stones.

The first Stonehenge proper was raised about 2800 BC, in the mid-Neolithic. Though modest, it was unusual in having a bank outside the ditch circle framed by timber posts set into holes (named after John Aubrey who recorded them in the 17th century). The monument then seems to have been left for a time, or used as a cemetery, before Phase II (*c.*2100 BC) began. Bronze-Age builders remodelled the site with a north-easterly alignment emphasized by the Avenue, a broad embankment extending 510 metres (1,600 feet) outside the ditch. They placed the four Station Stones in a rectangle, and formed the bluestones into two circles in the centre, each with an entrance looking along the Avenue. The bluestones had been floated by raft from the Preseli Hills of South Wales, upriver to Amesbury and

48

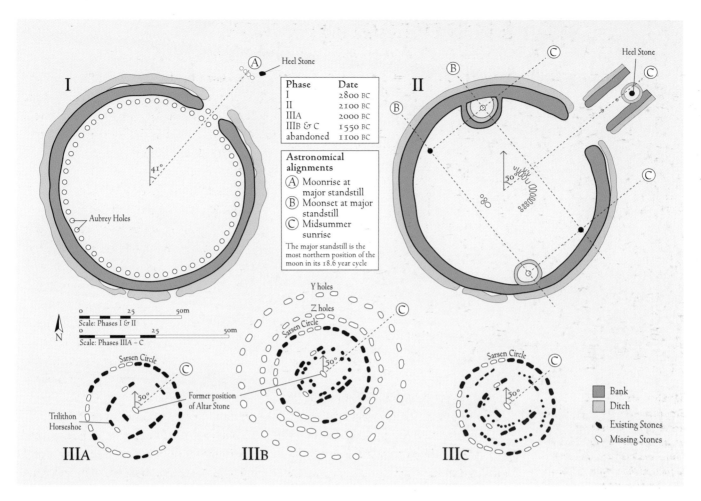

Phase	Date
I	2800 BC
II	2100 BC
IIIA	2000 BC
IIIB & C	1550 BC
abandoned	1100 BC

Astronomical alignments

Ⓐ Moonrise at major standstill
Ⓑ Moonset at major standstill
Ⓒ Midsummer sunrise

The major standstill is the most northern position of the moon in its 18.6 year cycle

Heel Stone

Aubrey Holes

41°

50°

0 25 50m
Scale: Phases I & II

0 25 50m
Scale: Phases IIIA – C

N

Y holes
Z holes
Sarsen Circle

Sarsen Circle

Trilithon Horseshoe

Former position of Altar Stone

Sarsen Circle

IIIA   IIIB   IIIC

■ Bank
■ Ditch
● Existing Stones
○ Missing Stones

then manhandled (probably on wooden sledges) to Stonehenge – a distance of 402 kilometres (nearly 250 miles).

Stonehenge's final makeover had three phases. The most spectacular, Phase IIIA (*c*.2000 BC), produced the giant Trilithon Horseshoe and the Sarsen Circle around it, with natural sandstone blocks weighing some 25 tonnes each, dragged from the Marlborough Downs. Phase IIIB (*c*.1550 BC) produced the Y and Z holes outside the sarsens. The bluestones were replaced in an oval within the Horseshoe, but were moved again (Phase IIIC) to their present site between the Trilithon Horseshoe and the Sarsen Circle.

But by 1100 BC, it seems that Stonehenge had been abandoned, subsequently to be targeted as a 'Druid stronghold' by the Romans, and then pillaged by locals for building stone.

STONEHENGE STEP-BY-STEP

A diagram showing the phases of Stonehenge's construction also reveals its astronomical alignments. The four Station Stones were arranged during Phase II in a huge rectangle. Its long sides indicate the moon setting in its extreme north position; the short sides indicate midsummer sunrise. Only at, or close to, the latitude of Stonehenge will a rectangle fulfil this dual function. The original Phase I entrance aligned with the most northerly rising of the moon, known as the 'major standstill'.

MYSTERIES AND ENIGMAS

STONEHENGE SURVIVORS
The most complete part of the outer circle of sarsens at Stonehenge, showing the surviving lintels, with stones of the Bluestone Circle inside it.

ANCIENT BRITAIN THROWS UP more questions than answers. Many surround Stonehenge, but few can be answered satisfactorily. Why, for example, is Stonehenge now a ruin? It was built soundly, the sarsen stones interlocked by chiselled tenon and mortise joints, and the uprights socketed firmly into the chalk. Solitary stones elsewhere still stand, so why did those at Stonehenge fall? One credible theory supposes that a Roman general deliberately 'slighted' (wrecked) the monument, believing it to be a stronghold of the Druids, whose religion and human sacrifice the Romans set out to destroy after invading Britain in AD 43.

And why was such prodigious effort made here? In 1858, it was noted that the Stonehenge bluestones were very like rocks in north Pembrokeshire. Proof came in 1923 that samples of dolerite and rhyolite from Stonehenge corresponded 'in the minutest detail' with rocks in the Preseli Hills. But why bring such massive boulders so far? It may be that the stones from the Preseli Hills were thought to have special religious value or healing properties. Seven stone circles still stand in the eastern Preseli Hills, and it is conceivable that Stonehenge's bluestones were originally erected there, before being moved to Wessex.

How was the monument made? Stone-building techniques have been tested to discover how such huge monoliths were shaped. Cracks in the stone may have had wooden wedges hammered into them. Wetting these would cause the wood to expand and so split the stone further. Heating with fire then dousing with water could also cause cracking. Hammering balls of extra-hard sarsen against the blocks, in the manner of modern demolition squads, may have trimmed or shattered the stones into shape. Ox-power would have been useful for moving and raising the megaliths – perhaps 20 oxen or 180 men to each large stone.

But how were the lintels put on top? The most practical lifting method was to erect a 'crib' of timber poles. Lifting one end of the stone allowed a pole to be slipped under first one end and then the other. Adding poles to the scaffolding inched the stone skywards until it was level with the top of the uprights. Then, with great care, the lintel was levered sideways to lock in place.

Ancient monuments were not speed-built. The secret behind Stonehenge's construction was that people worked at a regular pace for a very long time, using modest amounts of energy. It was a slow process; but time was on the side of the Stonehenge people. For succeeding generations, the pace of change would slowly accelerate, driven by a new technology forged in the furnace from metal ores: copper, tin and iron.

AERIAL VIEW OF STONEHENGE
A unique World Heritage Site, Stonehenge is now a place to be gazed upon from a safe distance, its mysteries 'explained' by aid of a tourist audio set. It may be that our own Bronze-Age ancestors, in the main, were also kept at a respectful distance by the presiding authorities.

BUSH BARROW MACE
Just south of Stonehenge is the Bush Barrow burial, dated around 2200 – 1900 BC. Here were found this stone mace, a gold lozenge, three large bronze daggers, one with a pommel inlaid with numerous tiny gold pins, and a 'baton' – all associated with the corpse of an adult male, once suggested as the architect of Stonehenge.

WHAT WENT ON AT STONEHENGE?

Theories as to the purpose of Stonehenge are many: a temple, a place of sacrifice, a solar calendar, an astronomical observatory. The medieval historian Geoffrey of Monmouth thought it a memorial to Britons slain by Saxon invaders. Modern scholars have seen it as a Neolithic solar/lunar computer, for predicting eclipses and other heavenly events. Recent studies suggest that ceremonial gatherings took place at the midwinter solstice, with beacons aflame on surrounding hills.

SILBURY HILL

'This temple ... when in perfection must have been the work of a very great and learned people.'

William Stukeley, 1743

SOFT ON TOP
Days of heavy rain in May 2000 caused the top of Silbury Hill to collapse. A shaft dug down from the summit of the mound in 1776–77 had subsided, leaving a pit about 20 metres (65 feet) deep.

SILBURY HILL is one of the enigmas of Ancient Britain, thrust up from the ancient Wessex landscape within sight of Avebury and Stonehenge, the two most important prehistoric sites in the country. Here, where ancient tracks and ridgeways converge, generations of travellers have passed by. The largest man-made prehistoric mound in Europe, Silbury Hill rises 40 metres (131 feet) above the Bath road. Close by is the West Kennet long barrow;

Avebury lies to the north and to the north-west stands Windmill Hill. This is the heart of the Wessex 'ritual landscape'.

Silbury Hill is rather like a giant wedding cake, built in a series of terraces, the first founded on rock and the six upper terraces made of chalk blocks. There are some visual parallels with the ziggurats (stepped pyramid-temples) of Mesopotamia, built at roughly the same

time (*c.*2800 BC). In the 17th century, John Aubrey wrote that 'the tradition only is that King Sil, or Zel as the country folk pronounce it, was buried here on horseback.' Legend spoke of a golden rider buried at the heart of the hill, but exploratory shafts (dug in 1776–77, 1849, 1867 and 1922) found no grave, and neither have more modern excavations, 1968–70. One imaginative theory claimed it as the tomb of an Egyptian astronomer-explorer, whose star-gazing headquarters were at Stonehenge.

In fact, what lay at Silbury Hill's centre was a cone-shape core of clay. From the plant and insect remains found in it, this was apparently prepared in high summer. The mound was perhaps linked with crop-gathering, a 'harvest hill' connected to a late-summer festival of gift-giving to the gods in the manner of the Celtic Lugnasad (Christian Lammastide). Its ritual nature continued for millennia, and in the 19th century,

local people walked to the top of the hill in springtime, on Palm Sunday.

Other harvest hills exist, though these are much smaller: Merlin's Mount at Marlborough in Wiltshire (landscaped into a garden in the 17th century), the Mount at Lewes in Sussex and Clifford Hill near Northampton. Silbury is unique in scale, if not purpose. Building it was a colossal effort for a local population unlikely to have numbered more than 1,000. The work probably took over a century, assuming that farmers could devote only part of the year to shifting chalk.

LOADS OF CHALK
A complex network of retaining chalk walls holds Silbury Hill in place. Superficially like a gigantic burial mound, it contains no burials. It is unique and unmissable, with its enormous bulk (325,000 cubic metres of chalk, stone and earth – an estimated 35 million basket-loads!).

HILL-BUILDING
An antler tine from Silbury Hill, excavated in 2001, one of many used by the hill-builders to dig out chalk.

53

SECRETS OF THE RINGS

GREAT MEGALITHS hauled upright into standing stone rings formed circles of invitation to some, but exclusion, perhaps, to others. Long after being set in place, these rings – so powerfully rich in meaning – were visited age upon age. Burial barrows made in number over periods of time can be found within walking distance of Stonehenge, producing a landscape richer in prehistoric remains than any other similar-sized area of Britain. This part of Wessex may well have had special significance – even before Stonehenge began to rise on the site of a late-Neolithic circular earthwork. (For a map of the south-west England 'ritual landscape', see the Wessex map on the front flap.)

STONES OF CALLANISH
Local tradition claims the stones are giants, turned to stone by Saint Kieran when they refused to become Christian.

RING OF GIANTS

Callanish (Callanais) on the Scottish island of Lewis is a stone circle from 2900–2600 BC. In a landscape of Neolithic fields and homes, 13 slender stones were set about a taller, central stone standing 4.75 metres (13.5 feet) high. Four avenues (one a double row, the others single stones) lead off roughly to the four compass points. From the southern avenue, the moon is seen skimming distant hilltops to mark the lunar cycle of 18.6 years.

LONG MEG AND
HER DAUGHTERS
*Long Meg and her Daughters
form a stone circle in Cumbria,
on the way to the Langdale axe
mines. Long Meg herself stands
3.7 metres (12 feet) high,
and the circle is 109 metres
(358 feet) across.*

Apart from its barrows, the ritual land-scape of Wessex included circular enclosures such as Robin Hood's Ball – a ceremonial meeting place, perhaps – and an avenue-route of parallel ditches called the Cursus. Then there were the four 'henge' monuments – Woodhenge, Coneybury, Durrington Walls and Stonehenge. And to the north, within easy walking distance (for Neolithic people), was another ritual complex: Silbury Hill and the stone circles of the Sanctuary, on Overton Hill, and Avebury, probably placed in position between the first and second stages of Stonehenge, around 2600 BC. The West Kennet Avenue of standing stones from Avebury to the Sanctuary, described as a temple, dates from around 2400 BC.

'Special' places elsewhere in Britain were also marked by stone and timber structures, rings and mounds. Those tending cattle or sheep, or harvesting wheat from the small fields around their houses, lived in the daily presence of these awesome monuments. Ceremonies focused on the mounds and stones delineated people's lives and beliefs – though in ways we do not fully understand. Five thousand years ago, these farmers had already seared the landscape with fire and flint axes, clearing woodland and letting their herds graze on young trees. They opened up a land once densely forested. Then, working together, they marked the rolling hills with monuments of stone, the material to which they owed their way of life.

ROLLRIGHT STONES
*Oxfordshire's famous megalithic
circle of some 70 stones stands
south-west of Banbury.*

TURNING FROM STONE

The Great Orme mine in North Wales, rediscovered in 1987 and now open to visitors, is the biggest Bronze-Age copper mine known in Europe, with tunnels more than 6 kilometres (4 miles) in extent. Miners dug for copper ore from around 1600 BC, hacking with bone and antler picks, and smashing rock with stone hammers. They used fire to split the rock, too, and laid wooden pipes to drain away water.

DAGGER DRAWN

Bronze daggers such as this were more reliable weapons than longer but easily broken bronze swords. This 33-centimetre (12-inch) long weapon was found in the owner's grave.

WESSEX PEOPLE WHO TROD the processional route between Avebury and the Sanctuary on Overton Hill, and the islanders on Lewis who peered at the moon from the stones of Callanish, used tools much like those of the first farmers – made from flint, antler, bone and wood. These were the materials on which human society had been built in Ancient Britain since the prehistoric Boxgrove people first hunted horses.

But by around 2300 BC, change was in the air, in the smoke from fires lit by Britain's first metalworkers. Copper, known as early as 6500 BC in Anatolia (Turkey), had first been used for making ornamental objects. Spain and Bulgaria led the way in European copper-making, as copper ore was smelted in a charcoal fire until a 'cake' of molten metal collected. Copper is soft enough to be hammered, but the cake could also be melted again, then poured into an open mould to make a flat axe or sword.

Bronze is a 1:8 alloy of tin and copper, presumably discovered by copper-workers experimenting with different mixtures of ores. Tin and copper were heated together to form a 'cake', which was then melted again for casting. Poured into a two-part mould, the molten bronze cooled, hardened, and was used to make more elaborate shapes for axes, daggers and spearheads.

Britain was well placed to exploit this new technology, with plentiful tin supplies in Cornwall, and abundant copper in the west and in Ireland. This put Britain at the heart of the Bronze Age, exporting tin, and the wealth of the Wessex Bronze Age marks the islands' new importance in the European economy. Copper was mined in Ireland by around 1800 BC, and in Wales by 1500 BC. In the 1840s, Victorian miners in North Wales discovered ancient workings 'containing stone hammers, quantities of bone and remains of fires'. The long-dead miners whose shafts they had stumbled on were not Roman (as was then assumed) but Ancient Britons.

Yet old Neolithic habits and skills died hard, as stone tools were still made for everyday wear and tear. Flint-working continued alongside bronze-working, dying out only around 500 BC. But bronze was now the most desirable material, especially for weapons. Bronze swords and daggers were sharper and less brittle than those of flint or copper. Bronze axes, thinner and more elegant than those of stone, were less prone to shatter. Bronze could also be decorated, and many axes were inscribed and polished. In the new 'Bronzed Britain', style was as valuable as utility.

CAST UPON THE WATERS

FLAG FEN
Within sight of Peterborough Cathedral, Flag Fen is a place where present and past merge almost seamlessly. Here have been found swords and other metalwork from the Bronze Age and Iron Age.

ANOTHER BRONZE-AGE community project was unearthed in 1982, when a mechanical digger gouged up some interesting waterlogged timbers from a Fenland ditch in Peterborough. Tests proved them to be 3,000 years old, the remains of late Bronze-Age hard labour, when people at Flag Fen sweated to drive 60,000 wooden posts into the boggy ground. Their worksite now forms one of Britain's prime Bronze-Age study areas.

Three thousand years ago, this was 'wet fen', crossed by a wooden causeway 7 metres (23 feet) wide, formed of poles and brushwood, pinned in place between the piles with wooden pegs. The path was of oak planks and brushwood, with a layer of sand and gravel on top. Either side of the fen lay fields and cattle enclosures, marked by ditches and thorn hedges. The enclosures had corner entrances, the simplest way to drive stock in and out.

Flag Fen's waters were evidently used to deposit offerings, including pottery, bronze daggers, and swords of two styles: a narrow thrusting blade and a leaf-shaped slashing weapon. So many swords

HEART OF OAK
The Dover boat's oak timbers, now conserved.

have been found that most men must have owned at least one. Flag Fen also yielded the earliest wheel known in Britain. Made about 1300 BC, it was a solid wooden wheel, made in three sections of alder held together with oak braces and ash pegs.

People here lived between land and water and, as water levels rose, may have been forced onto higher ground. Perhaps they built the causeway as a symbolic defence against flooding, a place of offering to ancestors and gods, in a bid to hold onto their farmland. Similar causeways have been found at Shinewater near Eastbourne in Sussex and at Fiskerton near Lincoln. And throwing metal into water, as an offering, continued well into the Iron Age.

Water played another important part in Bronze-Age British life. As well as its causeway, Fiskerton is notable for two boats made from hollowed-out oaks. Log boats are fairly common (over a hundred are known, and some seem to have been sunk on purpose, hardly used – perhaps as a ritual offering). Boats and rafts transported heavy cargo (such as building stones) and acted as river ferries. The most intriguing Bronze-Age boat of all, found at Dover, was big enough to have crossed the Channel.

SHEARING KIT
Bronze shears from Flag Fen and the wooden holder with which they were found. Other bronze objects from this 3,000-year-old site include swords, daggers, a carpenter's gouge, and a flesh-hook for lifting chunks of meat from a large cooking pot.

HOMES AND FARMS

REBUILT HOME
A reconstructed Iron-Age house, from Butser Ancient Farm near Petersfield in Hampshire. It was windowless, with a deeply sloping thatched roof to keep out wind and rain. There was no chimney either. Smoke curled out through the roof, creating a draught to keep the fire burning without creating a 'pea-soup' fog inside.

QUICK TO ABSORB new skills, Iron-Age people adjusted farming and building techniques to the land where they lived. Farmers ploughed small, squarish fields, measuring around 120 by 80 metres (130 by 90 yards) to sow cereals. Their main crops were wheat, barley, oats and rye, along with peas, beans, lentils, vetch, and flax for linen. They also coppiced trees to provide easily cut poles for building, fencing and fuel.

Like their Neolithic and Bronze-Age forebears, Iron-Age farmers kept cattle for food, milk and hides, as well as pigs and sheep. Sheep wool was woven into weatherproof clothes, dyed with plants to produce bright colours and patterns. Oxen were bred for heavy pulling but small, wiry horses were prized for light farm work, warfare and racing. The people of Britain relished horse-trading, and the quality of their decorative horse-gear reflects their regard for the animal. Dogs were kept as pets, as guards and for hunting. Chickens, originally domesticated in Asia, may have pecked about on Iron-Age farms, but quite how and when domestic poultry, including ducks and geese, came to Britain is not certain.

Around 100 BC, more woodland was cut down. Farmers drained heavy clay soils and formed bigger cattle herds. They used iron ploughs, and may have practised crop rotation. The countryside created in Britain by the time of the late Iron Age was to remain familiar up until the very recent past: woods, meadows, and fields within ditches, walls or hedges. On the slopes of the chalky South Downs, traces of Celtic fields, cattle folds, droveways, ditches and settlement enclosures linger still.

Iron-Age farmers in Gaul, noted Julius Caesar in the 1st century BC, chose to live 'surrounded by forest … for to avoid the heat they generally seek the neighbourhood of woods and rivers.' Excessive heat may not have been a British problem in the late Iron Age, when the climate was much as it is today. Farming families lived, together with their stock, inside a farmstead protected by a bank and ditch. Settlements varied: unwalled villages; hill forts, some as big as towns; sites of religious gatherings; a few industrial areas such as salt works in coastal East Anglia, or trading centres such as Hengistbury Head, Dorset. There were villages of stone houses, like Chysauster in Cornwall (where every home had a garden) and homes on stilts over water, as at the Lake Village in Glastonbury, Somerset.

Unlike most of their cross-Channel neighbours, Britons liked round houses with cone-shaped, sloping roofs made of reed, straw or heather thatch. Some British homes were over 10 metres (33 feet) across, roomy enough for 30 adults. Wattle walls of woven twigs were plastered and weatherproofed by clay daub. But some builders walled their homes with upright wooden planks, or with stones. There was a doorway but no window. Animal hides added warmth and comfort to the home, which was centrally heated by the hearth-fire of peat or logs, while the family stew slow-cooked in a heavy iron cauldron suspended above it.

BEANS ON TOAST?
Two staple crops in Iron-Age Britain were emmer wheat and beans, such as these grown at Butser Ancient Farm.

RANKING SOCIETY

IRON-AGE PEOPLE LIVED in family communities (or clans), within wider tribal groups whose pattern of alliances constantly shifted. A king or chief, with a powerful tribal council of nobles, led a society in which a person identified primarily with family and clan community, rather than the territory in which they lived. Society had become more markedly hierarchical, and among Europeans 'clientship' was a way to reinforce social position. 'Underdogs' served an aristocratic chieftain in return for his protection – or for work, in the case of a craftsman. Clients might belong to other tribes; or whole tribes could become clients of stronger communities.

While most Britons farmed peacefully, people at the top increasingly won status in war. Victory for an Iron-Age war-leader, in battles usually no more than skirmishes or raids on near-neighbours, brought him followers seeking a share of the spoil. Warlords vied to show hospitality and public generosity by distributing gifts at a tribal feast, often wild and drunken, where hierarchy was confirmed. Men sat in a circle, ranked in order around the person foremost in wealth, birth or battle honour. Status might then be tested. For example, the 'hero's portion' of meat was awarded to the bravest warrior, but should another claim it, fighting to the death meant the 'best man' won.

Britain was moving into a new way of life from around 500 BC, closer to the medieval and away from the prehistoric. Villages were growing, some on the verge of becoming small towns, with more specialist tradesmen like the wheelwright. There were potters, jewellers, coiners,

CHYSAUSTER SETTLEMENT
Some Iron-Age villages had stone-walled houses, arranged in 'cells', like these at Chysauster in Cornwall, without an outer wall-defence. Stoutly built homes such as these could last for several generations.

seafarers, salt-makers, swordsmiths and goldsmiths, bards, musicians. Craftsmen, producing the tools, weapons and decorated metalwork that formed much of a community's wealth, had high rank. At the bottom of society's heap were slaves, whose value might equal a container of wine consumed at the tribal feast.

Among Celtic peoples, priests guarded tribal identity, maintaining law, learning and custom. The highest levels of society were reserved for men only, yet European evidence suggests that Celtic noblewomen may have been more influential than those in the Greco-Roman world. Julius Caesar noted that in Gaul, man and wife pooled equal amounts of money and at death the survivor inherited all. He also remarked that in Britain some women shared several husbands.

What were these late Iron-Age Britons like? Men were mostly clean-shaven, though warriors of high rank

SLAVE CHAIN
An iron slave chain from Wales, found with other metal objects in a peat bog. Slaves were at the bottom of Iron-Age society, some captured in war, although others may have been born into slavery.

wore droopy moustaches, and some had short beards. Romans were struck by 'Celtic hairstyles', liberally plastered with lime wash and shaped to look like a lion's mane. Women wore long skirts but the men's trousers were un-Mediterranean, breeches having probably originated on the Eurasian steppes among horse-riding Scythian and Iranian nomads. Fostering out children seems to have been a widespread custom, at least among the nobility/warrior caste. Caesar comments 'they do not allow their sons to approach them in public unless they have grown up to the age of military service, and they think it a disgrace for a boy under this age to sit in public within sight of his father.'

OFFERINGS AND SACRIFICES

RITUAL AND MAGIC linked Iron-Age peoples to their gods, the Celtic spirits of nature haunting wooded groves or sparkling pools. Rites were performed at these shrines and holy places, but also in religious enclosures or temples. Much of what we know about Iron-Age religion comes from Roman sources, usually hostile. Ritual was guarded by Druids, tribal priests whose name was related to 'oak' and who were later the object of Roman fear and loathing.

LOST LAKE
Llyn Cerrig Bach, a sacred lake on Anglesey, North Wales, where offerings to the spirits were made by throwing into the water iron weapons, tools, slave chains and animal bones. More than a hundred objects were recovered from Llyn Cerrig Bach in the 1940s, during construction of an RAF airfield.

GRIM DEATH

The Roman writer Pliny described human sacrifice: '**Clad in a white robe, the priest ascends the [oak] tree and cuts the mistletoe with a golden sickle ... They then kill the victims.**' Other forms of human sacrifice aroused equal horror in the Romans, for they involved '**figures of immense size, whose limbs, woven out of twigs, they fill with living men and set on fire.**'

Found in a dried-up bog in 1984, this young man – knocked out, strangled, stabbed in the throat and flung face down into a boggy pool – seems to have suffered ritual sacrifice. He may have taken a mistletoe potion, possibly supplied by Druids, shortly before a death that could have been voluntary, to seek the gods' aid against the Romans.

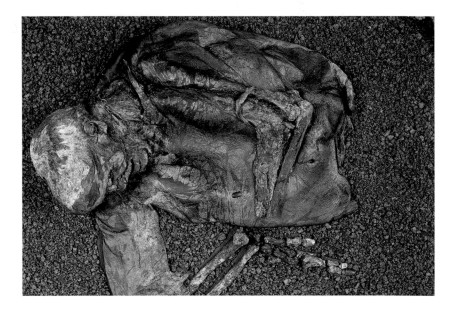

Central to religious rites were trees and water sources where offerings were made to the sacred spirit of the place. The Roman writer Lucan, appalled at the thought of rotting wooden idols and branches smeared with human blood, observed that sacrificial death had to fit a god's particular demands. The god Taranis required burning, for example; Teutates, drowning; while Esus' victims were hanged. Certainly there is evidence of people being placed in water as offerings of some kind; the 'Lindow Man' burial in Cheshire is one example.

Iron-Age deities were linked to place and nature. Deities known from inscriptions include Sul, goddess of the hot spring at Bath; Epona, the horse goddess; and the water goddess Elen. Dedications to Maponus are found around Hadrian's Wall and Nodens in Gloucestershire. Some gods were linked in triads; others were shape-shifters, transforming into animals. There was a belief in life beyond death, after which, so Druids taught, the soul passed to another body.

Feasts and festivals, including sacrifices, were held on a small scale at farmsteads and on a larger scale at communal centres such as the hill forts. There were also 'shrines' or temples (two were found at Heathrow and Stansted), and hoards of gold, such as that from Snettisham in Norfolk. Essendon in Hertfordshire produced a coin-hoard that was probably

associated with a spring. Lakes also attracted offerings – a spectacular find of weapons, horse harness and vehicle fittings came from Llyn Cerrig Bach in Anglesey.

There were four great Celtic seasonal festivals. The year began with Samain at the end of October, on a night when magic burst loose into the world. This was the turn of the year, when farm animals were slaughtered before winter. Imbolc heralded lambing, in February, and Beltane in May saw the cattle sent out to graze, passing between lighted fires. Lugnasad fell at the start of August, as crops ripened.

ELEGANT DAGGER
The Cookham dagger, with its equally elegant sheath, was found in the River Thames, Berkshire.

IRON MEN

'The whole race ... is madly fond of war, high spirited and quick to battle.'

The Greek historian Strabo, on the Celts

THE CELTS, EUROPE's 'men of iron' from the 6th century BC, had been long predominant in west and central Europe – until confronted by Roman power. Celtic battle strategy was tried and trusted. First came the terrifying display – screaming war cries, clashing swords on shields, blasting horns and trumpets. Then, hair streaming, the warriors charged, often naked but for sword belt and gold neck torc (a horse-shoe-shaped ornament). Across Europe, Celts had fought amongst themselves, tribe against tribe, champion against champion, competing for glory.

In Britain, this Iron-Age machismo was demonstrated by raiding expeditions to steal cattle, women, slaves and anything else of value from their neighbours. Booty won increased tribal wealth and its leader's prestige. More formidable weapons, notably long slashing swords, and horse harnesses, were adopted by British warriors who – judging from the increased quantity and quality of horse-harness grave goods – were more mobile than their ancestors. The sword was

MARTIAL ART
Iron-Age metalworkers created designs of timeless artistry, including this decorated shield boss fished from the River Thames at Wandsworth. It was made in the 2nd or 1st century BC.

WELSH COUNTRY LIVING
At Din Lligwy, Anglesey, in North Wales, are the remains of an Iron-Age country estate with several buildings enclosed by a stone wall. This circular house, which had steps up to the entrance, was probably the main building.

usually carried across the warrior's back. Unarmoured combat must have been bloody: excavations at Danebury hill fort uncovered the remains of at least ten men who had suffered battle wounds, half of them skull slashes.

Warriors were interred with their war gear – a fairly typical grave at Owslebury in Hampshire was of a man buried with a sword on his right, a spear on his left, and his shield (wood and leather with a metal boss or centrepiece, which alone survived) laid over his body.

In defence of hearth and home, less costly weapons proved useful. Piles of pebbles found in hill-fort ramparts show that

SWORD SURVIVOR
Few iron swords survive 2,000 years or more of exposure. Their rusted remains can only hint at the craftsmanship that forged a brightly glittering, newly polished weapon.

slingers were on guard. They selected missiles with care, often from some distance away, preferring stones about 3 centimetres (just over 1 inch) across. The sling itself, made of leather, was cheap but effective, hurling volleys of stones from the hilltop as far as 50 metres (55 yards) or more to ward off attackers.

BOAR PROTECTOR
The boar was believed to have protective powers, and this little bronze boar dating from the 1st century BC might once have adorned a warrior's helmet.

81

HIGH ON A HILL

THE BRITISH BUILT HILL FORTS to defend their herds and families, and as centres of local administration and trade. Hill forts were an effective deterrent to 'neighbourly aggression': surrounded by rings of ditches and earth banks, topped by wooden stakes and with a twisting entrance difficult to storm unscathed, they looked impregnable.

Britain's network of hill forts was most dense in south-central Britain, from the Channel coast to North Wales. Behind their banks and their ditches, hill forts provided places of safety at times of inter-tribal warfare, but were much more than armed camps for warriors. Danebury in Hampshire and Maiden Castle, Dorset, for example, were big and busy settlements in which people lived, worked, traded, stored produce and kept their animals. Tribal centres, and probably markets, they sucked in people from the surrounding area, for the countryside round about seems to have been used for farming rather than housing.

Some fortified sites in southern Britain, such as those at Bigbury in Kent and Wheathampstead in Hertfordshire, had by the 2nd–1st centuries BC evolved into *oppida*, the Latin name given by Caesar

FROM AGE TO AGE
Originally a Neolithic causewayed enclosure, the hill fort of Hambledon Hill in Dorset remained in occupation into the Iron Age. It is among the largest ancient settlements in Britain.

'By the first century BC, over great tracts of Britain, it would have been impossible to have looked out across a landscape without seeing dozens of farmsteads.'

Professor Barry Cunliffe, Iron Age Britain

to sites in Gaul that were larger than a village or farmstead. They were bigger than most hill forts, and less forbidding to visitors. Such centres of British regional authority as Camulodunum (Colchester) were often but not always tribal capitals. *Oppida* grew in number as Celtic society became more centralized, with fewer, stronger tribes. They were on the way to becoming towns.

By the time of the Romans' arrival in the 1st century BC, Britain's population may have reached 4 or 5 million – perhaps five times greater than when Stonehenge was being built. Much more energy was going into 'production' – of pottery, ironwork, farming – and much less on building monumental structures. Hill forts were now the biggest human influence on the

landscape, succeeding the ancient landmarks as a way to demonstrate the power and confidence of the builders.

Inside their settlements, people followed traditional crafts, using specialist tools for specialist jobs: wheel-making for carts and chariots, boat-building from wooden planks, and forging swords. Local potters produced rough utensils for everyday use, while finer wares were traded on pack animals across the country. Most households probably attempted some, if not all, everyday tasks themselves, especially spinning, weaving, basketry and pottery.

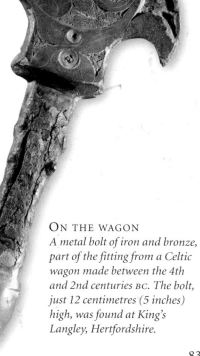

ON THE WAGON
A metal bolt of iron and bronze, part of the fitting from a Celtic wagon made between the 4th and 2nd centuries BC. The bolt, just 12 centimetres (5 inches) high, was found at King's Langley, Hertfordshire.

MAIDEN CASTLE

'...one of the finest and largest Iron-Age hill forts in Europe, its banks enclose an area the size of 50 football pitches, which would have been home to about 200 families.'

English Heritage, present custodian of Maiden Castle

MAIDEN CASTLE, just outside Dorchester in Dorset, is the largest hill fort in Britain, covering some 47 acres. Its earth ramparts are still over 6 metres (20 feet) high in places, despite 2,000 years of wind and rain, plus the footfall of countless human visitors. Such an immense fortress must have looked fearsome to any attacking force, yet it fell to the Romans in AD 43 or 44.

Like most places in Ancient Britain, Maiden Castle passed through stages of occupation and use. First occupied during the Neolithic period, a causewayed camp was built within a ditch and bank at the eastern end of what is now a vast oval, about half the size of Maiden Castle today. Later additions included a 'bank barrow' almost 400 metres (440 yards) long (about 3500 BC) and a small, early Iron-Age fort (about 600 BC) which was later enlarged.

The fort was extended in the 300s BC by adding a village, which later spread to the west. The two gated entrances to the camp (east and west) were reinforced defensively by projecting earthworks, and in the 1st century BC the defences seem to have been strengthened again, perhaps by

WITHIN THESE WALLS
The banked walls of Maiden Castle have stood for over 2,500 years. Hill forts were tribal centres, refuges and meeting places. They dominated the landscape of southern Britain.

DENIED ENTRY
Maiden Castle in its prime was a strongly defended settlement, as this reconstruction shows. Villagers living on the hilltop must have felt secure against all comers behind its formidable barriers. The hill fort's entrances were designed to make direct attack difficult, and such massive defences symbolized the community's strength and prestige.

refugees from Brittany where the Romans were attacking the Veneti, a seafaring tribe with close ties to Britain. At its most formidable, the fort had three concentric rings of ditches and ramparts, with a wooden palisade along the top of the inner defence. The entrances through each ring were offset, so that an attacking force could be jammed into a 'killing zone' within the ditch, at the mercy of stones, spears and arrows pelted from the ramparts.

∽

After the Roman invasion of Britain in AD 43, the 2nd Augusta Legion, led by Vespasian (later emperor of Rome) marched west to attack Maiden Castle, a stronghold of the powerful Durotriges tribe. Despite its ramparts, the hill fort fell to a determined Roman assault, the defence weakened perhaps by tribal rivalries that so often beset Iron-Age Britain. Sir Mortimer Wheeler, excavator of Maiden Castle in 1934–37, believed the Romans massacred the Britons, and that a 'war cemetery' marked the burial of men, women and children. Modern thinking has thrown doubt on this version of events (the cemetery is now thought to have been for local civilian use), though

evidence of battle, such as a Roman catapult bolt embedded in a victim's spine, leaves little doubt as to the violence of Iron-Age siege warfare.

∽

The Romans 'slighted', or razed, the age-old defences, and the people of the hill left the high ground for new-town life in nearby Durnovaria (Dorchester). A small Roman-British temple, its foundations still visible, was built on the site about AD 370–380. The great fort itself was left to grazing sheep and wheeling birds, the ploughman, the archaeologist, and the sighing of the wind.

MAIDEN CASTLE TODAY
Seen from the air, the Dorset hill fort still retains its power to impress, even without the buildings that stood in its centre over 2,000 years ago.

CHARIOT CHIEFS

RULERS OF THE MOST powerful Iron-Age tribes – the Iceni, Catuvellauni and Atrebates of the south and east – lived like kings and took their riches with them to the grave. In East Yorkshire, thousands of Celtic burials, dating mainly from the 3rd–1st centuries BC, were made within a square ditch, from which earth was heaped up into a barrow or tumulus over the grave. Some have wagons inside, or chariots; others had spears hurled into them; one yielded an early coat of mail. These Yorkshire graves were in the tribal area of the Parisii, a people who also lived in Gaul and who gave their name to France's modern capital.

ANCIENT EMBLEM
Uffington's White Horse is etched in the turf below Uffington Castle, a hill fort on the Berkshire Downs lying on a spine of the Ridgeway, one of the ancient trackways crossing southern England.

Since they were like burials found in northern France and Belgium, the Yorkshire graves were once thought to be evidence of invaders, from across the North Sea. Certainly there seems to have been contact. On the other hand, maybe the local Yorkshire elite decided to copy grand funeral customs they had seen on a visit to the Continental Parisii, or perhaps

the Parisii brought the observance with them. Chariot burials like that at Wetwang Slack in Yorkshire reveal a two-wheeled vehicle with its driver. Although similar graves have been found outside Yorkshire, and in Lincolnshire and Edinburgh, they seem to be isolated cases.

Vehicles buried in this way were not all war chariots. Some appear to have been specially built funeral carriages, carefully dismantled in the tomb. Their design looks too heavy and box-like for the hurly-burly of the battlefield, but they

THE WHITE HORSE

Ten 'White Horses' prance across Wiltshire's chalk downland. All may appear prehistoric, yet only one – the White Horse of Uffington – pre-dates the 18th century. John Aubrey thought the Uffington horse was Saxon, and others that it marked King Alfred's victory over the Vikings at Ashdown in AD 878. But tests in 2004 suggest that the horse was cut in the chalk between 1380 and 555 BC. Other chalk figures in southern England – including the Cerne Abbas Giant in Dorset and Sussex's Long Man of Wilmington – are 'modern', probably dating from the 1650s.

'First they drive in all directions hurling spears. Generally they manage to throw the ranks of their foes into confusion, purely by the terror caused by their galloping horses and the din of the chariot wheels.'

Julius Caesar, on meeting British war chariots in 55 BC

must have dignified the death rites of their owners, and enhanced the prestige of his or her family.

The fighting chariot was a lightweight, high-speed vehicle. Roman sources describe how warriors leaped down from their chariots to fight on foot, while the drivers galloped off, waiting to dash back and pick up their warriors (who might be brandishing the trophy of an enemy's head) for duty elsewhere on the field. Romans were impressed by the skill of British charioteers, who could 'run along the pole, stand on the yoke and get back into the chariot with incredible speed'.

In 55 BC, the British general and chieftain Cassivellaunus mustered 4,000 chariots to face the Romans. It took some time for the invaders to deal with a 'hit and run' enemy, but chariots were already obsolete and (unfortunately for them) the Britons saw no need to modernize. In AD 61, when Boudicca led the revolt of the Iceni against Roman conquest, her warriors employed the same tactics as their great-grandfathers. The British queen raced about in a chariot, hurling insults at the enemy and rousing her followers to roaring defiance. Families in wagons watched from the rear, as chariots thundered into battle – in a final flourish that ended in crushing defeat. No more would chariot charges win British victories.

CHARIOT BURIAL

This grave at Gorton-on-the-Wolds, Yorkshire, contains two wheels from a chariot, along with the skeleton. Of the hundreds of graves in this area, mainly 3rd–1st centuries BC, some contain wagons or chariots, others weapons and one produced an early example of chain-mail armour.

Iron-Age culture

A DISTINCTIVE IRON-AGE 'Celtic' style, forged by the 5th century BC, was first discovered at La Tène on Lake Neuchâtel in Switzerland. By the 3rd century BC, La Tène culture had come to Britain, bringing its characteristic abstract decoration of curling lines, a typically 'Celtic' art style. In Iron-Age Britain, high honour was the right of artists, the pattern-weavers of intricate designs in metal, music or poetry. Tribal poets were the bards, who preserved their people's history in age-old recitations. At Celtic feasts the bards lauded their own, lampooned their foes, and raised morale after defeat or victory.

By 300 BC, craftsmen in Britain were creating scabbards, shield bosses, mirrors, weapons, horse harnesses and torcs decorated in the geometric forms they loved. They used iron compasses to create decorative circles, spirals, whorls and ellipses in interlaced patterns filled with engraved lines or dots. They traced twirly plant tendril motifs, adding stylized human or animal faces – often the geese and hares they thought had magical properties. Other motifs are familiar, such as the three-legged triskele, emblem of the Isle of Man. The La Tène art style, lost elsewhere in Europe at the Roman conquest, survived on the western fringes of Wales, Scotland and Ireland, where Roman influence was minimal.

No bardic poetry was written down in Iron-Age Britain. Nor is there any ancient writing to confirm that Iron-Age peoples of the British Isles included Celts, but a trail of Celtic place names exists in Britain, for natural features such as hills and rivers (Thames, Avon and Trent). Modern county names derive from old tribal groups, such as Devon's Dumnonii and their sub-group, the Cornovii of Cornwall. Kent is Celtic, as is Elmet, in Yorkshire,

POLISHED MIRROR
Iron-Age people were fastidious and proud of their appearance. This polished bronze mirror was made in the 1st century AD (around the time of the Roman conquest of southern Britain). The swirling design is typical of the last two centuries BC.

'They wear ornaments of gold, torcs on their necks, and bracelets on their arms and wrists … it is this vanity which makes them unbearable in victory and so completely cast down in defeat …'

A Roman view of the Celtic character

NORFOLK TORC
In 1948 a Norfolk ploughman turned up what he thought was part of a brass bedstead. It was in fact an Iron-Age gold torc or neck-ring. Further finds came to light over the next 45 years: 75 complete torcs, the remains of 100 more, plus coins and metal ingots. Why the Snettisham Hoard, now in the British Museum, was buried remains a mystery. Some of its coins date from around 70 BC.

a British tribal territory until the 7th century. To this day, two forms of Celtic are spoken in the islands: one comprises Irish, Scots and Manx Gaelic; the other, Welsh and Cornish. And, locked in folk memory, echoes of ancient songs celebrating heroism and disaster have passed down into legend.

The largest hoard of gold and silver coins from pre-Roman Britain, unearthed in

Leicestershire in 2003, contained 3,000 coins and was a treasure-gift for the gods, perhaps, rather than a thief's abandoned booty. The same site also revealed a shattered silver-gilt iron helmet, of Roman style, which must have belonged to a high-ranking Roman soldier, possibly a Briton who had joined the Romans before the invasion of AD 43. Ambitious Britons no doubt saw Roman Europe as the place to do business and make contacts.

BRONZE BULL
The animal on which this ornament was modelled could have been a plough-ox or, more likely, the fierce wild aurochs of the forest.

89

ECHOES OF
ANCIENT BRITAIN

> *'The treasures of time lie … in Urnes, Coins and Monuments,*
> *scarce below the roots of some vegetables …'*
>
> Sir Thomas Browne, Urn Burial, 1658

SIR THOMAS BROWNE WAS among the first to convey the ups and downs of amateur archaeology. In 1667 he stumbled across 'some Urnes' (funeral urns) in Brampton, Norfolk. 'While the workmen made several ditches, they fell upon divers Urnes, but … carelessly digging, they broke all they met with and finding nothing but Ashes, or burnt Cinders, they scattered what they found.' The fate of these cremation urns, which were in fact Saxon, has been shared by many relics of the past. Much of Ancient Britain has been lost for ever: dug up, ploughed under, built over.

It was during the Renaissance of the 1400s–1500s that people began taking an interest in antiquities and, through them, in archaeology. Then, the discovery in the 18th century of Pompeii's buried ruins inspired hope that similar wonders might lie beneath British fields and villages. Nationalism played a part, too: the first students of Stonehenge were proud that Britain had such an ancient history, even if the Ancient Britons who built it were only 'two or three degrees less savage than the Americans' (John Aubrey, writing in the 17th century). By the 19th century, the prehistoric past seemed a bewildering mixture of dinosaur bones, cave men, Druids and bones in barrows. But as careful excavation gradually replaced treasure-seekers' destructive digging,

technology has thrown light on the shadows. There is now a time-frame against which to set what we know.

Yet the reminders of an ancient past lie around us – landscape, stones, fields and paths, as well as small, everyday objects to be found in gardens, on beaches, or afternoon walks – a fossil in a lump of chalk, a piece of worked flint, a stone arrowhead, a shard of pottery, a coin. From such fragments, archaeologists and palaeontologists reconstruct solid reality, and reveal how close are our connections to prehistory. We are direct heirs of the people who shaped stone tools, scratched art on rock, mastered bronze-casting and iron-forging, and who built still-awesome monuments of stone. Conserving what is left, to inform the present and to preserve the evidence for future generations, is a constant challenge.

CAPE OF GOLD
The gleaming gold Mold cape, a breathtaking survivor from the Bronze Age, c.1900–1600 BC. Beaten from a single ingot, and then painstakingly decorated, the cape, found in Flintshire, North Wales, is unique in form and design and one of the finest examples of prehistoric sheet-gold working.

INTO THE SUNSET
Stonehenge at sunset, when the glowing sun breathes warmth into the mellowed stones.

93

BACK TO THE BEGINNING

UNCOVERING TIME'S
TEXTURE
*An archaeologist at work on an
Iron-Age site prior to construction of the high-speed rail link
through Kent. Building work
both uncovers, and destroys,
evidence of the long-hidden past.*

THE PEOPLE OF ANCIENT BRITAIN lived with nature in a way that we cannot recapture, their lives minutely affected by changing seasons and daily weather variations. We can only imagine what their lives were like from revisiting their haunts: peering into the dark emptiness of a dank, eerie barrow; tracing the bark on ancient trees; striding an age-old ridgeway path; watching the sunrise at Stonehenge; surveying the surrounding land from a hilltop fort. Our urban, crowded world would be alien to a Neolithic hunter. Genetically our match, he would outstrip us easily in his own environment.

Most people today experience Ancient Britain as tourists to famous relics and landmarks, and as visitors to museum collections. Many are introduced to archaeology through television or family outings to a 'dinosaur park' or 'Iron-Age village'. Some, finding themselves alone

in a field before a slab-stone tomb, may feel a spine-tingling shiver as they reflect in the silence on life and death over hundreds of generations – the chain of history that links us to our ancestors.

MIDSUMMER REVELS
*Modern 'Druids' and other
interested visitors celebrate the
summer solstice.*

94

INDEX